Pebble Plus

Exploremos la galaxia/Exploring the Galaxy

Júpiter/Jupiter

por/by Thomas K. Adamson

Traducción/Translation: Martín Luis Guzmán Ferrer, Ph.D.
Editor Consultor/Consulting Editor: Dra. Gail Saunders-Smith

James Gerard, Consultant
Aerospace Education Specialist, NASA
Kennedy Space Center, Florida

Capstone
press

Mankato, Minnesota

Pebble Plus is published by Capstone Press
151 Good Counsel Drive, P.O. Box 669, Mankato, Minnesota 56002
http://www.capstone-press.com

1 2 3 4 5 6 11 10 09 08 07 06

Library of Congress Cataloging-in-Publication Data
Adamson, Thomas K.
    [Jupiter. Spanish & English]
    Júpiter = Jupiter / by Thomas K. Adamson.
    p. cm.—(Pebble plus: Exploremos la galaxia = Exploring the galaxy)
    Includes index.
    English and Spanish.
    ISBN-13: 978-0-7368-5879-3 (hardcover)
    ISBN-10: 0-7368-5879-2 (hardcover)
    1. Jupiter (Planet)—Juvenile literature. I. Title.
QB661.A3318 2004
523.45—dc22   2005019041

Summary: Simple text and photographs describe the planet Jupiter.

Editorial Credits
Mari C. Schuh, editor; Kia Adams, designer; Alta Schaffer, photo researcher; Eida del Risco, Spanish copy editor; Jenny Marks, bilingual editor

Photo Credits
Digital Vision, 5 (Venus)
John Foster/Photo Researchers, 20-21
NASA, 1, 4 (Pluto), 9, 11, 12-13, 15 (Jupiter), 17, 19; JPL, 5 (Jupiter); JPL/Caltech, 5 (Uranus)
PhotoDisc, Inc., cover, 4 (Neptune), 5 (Earth, Sun, Saturn, Mars, and Mercury), 15 (Earth)
Photri-Microstock/NASA, 6-7

Note to Parents and Teachers

The Exploremos la galaxia/Exploring the Galaxy series supports national standards related to earth and space science. This book describes Jupiter in both English and Spanish. The photographs support early readers and language learners in understanding the text. Repetition of words and phrases helps early readers and language learners learn new words. This book also introduces early readers to subject-specific vocabulary words, which are defined in the Glossary section. Early readers may need assistance to read some words and to use the Table of Contents, Glossary, Internet Sites, and Index sections of the book.

Table of Contents

Tabla de contenidos

Jupiter

Jupiter is the fifth planet
from the Sun. Jupiter
is the largest planet
in the solar system.

Júpiter

Júpiter es el quinto planeta
a partir del Sol. Júpiter
es el planeta más grande
del sistema solar.

4

The Solar System/El sistema solar

Jupiter/Júpiter

Sun/El Sol

Features

Jupiter is made mostly of gases. It is called a gas giant.

Características

En gran parte Júpiter está formado por gases. Se le llama un gigante gaseoso.

7

Jupiter has no solid surface.
A spacecraft cannot land
on Jupiter. But it can study
Jupiter's gases up close.

Júpiter no tiene una superficie sólida.
Una nave espacial no puede aterrizar
en Júpiter. Pero sí puede estudiar
de cerca los gases de Júpiter.

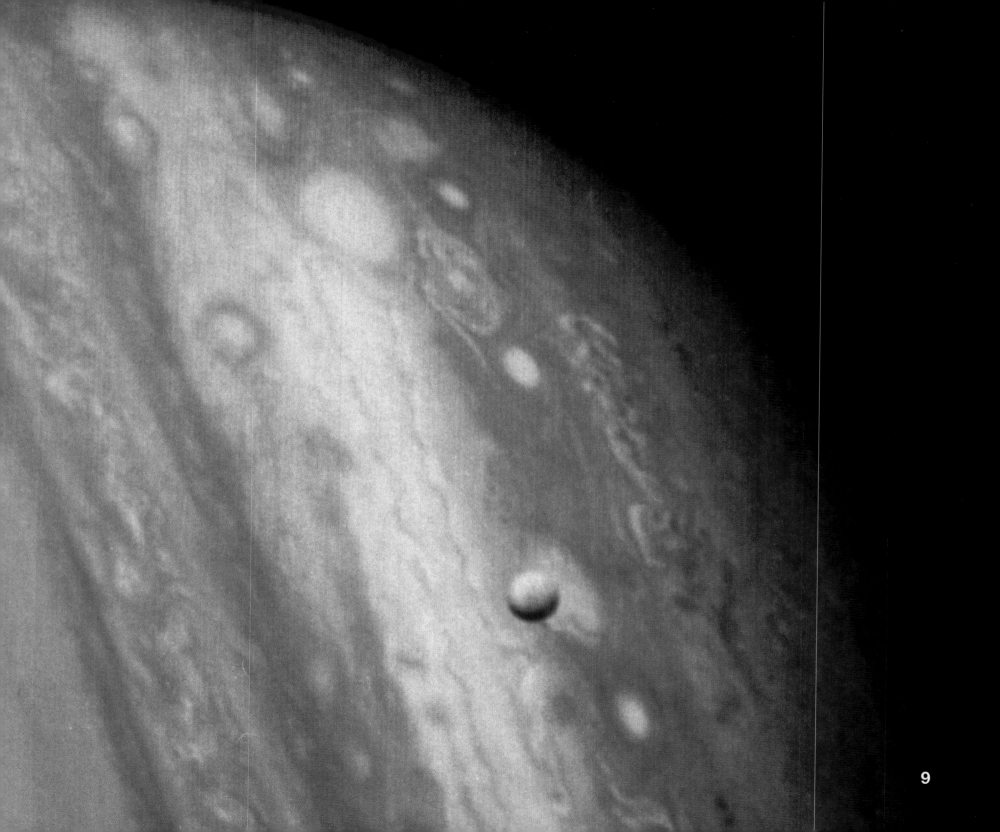

9

Orange and white clouds
circle Jupiter. The clouds
are thick.

Nubes anaranjadas y blancas
giran alrededor de Júpiter.
Las nubes son densas.

11

The Great Red Spot is
a large storm on Jupiter.
The storm is twice
as big as Earth.

La Gran Mancha Roja es
una enorme tormenta en Júpiter.
La tormenta es el doble
del tamaño de la Tierra.

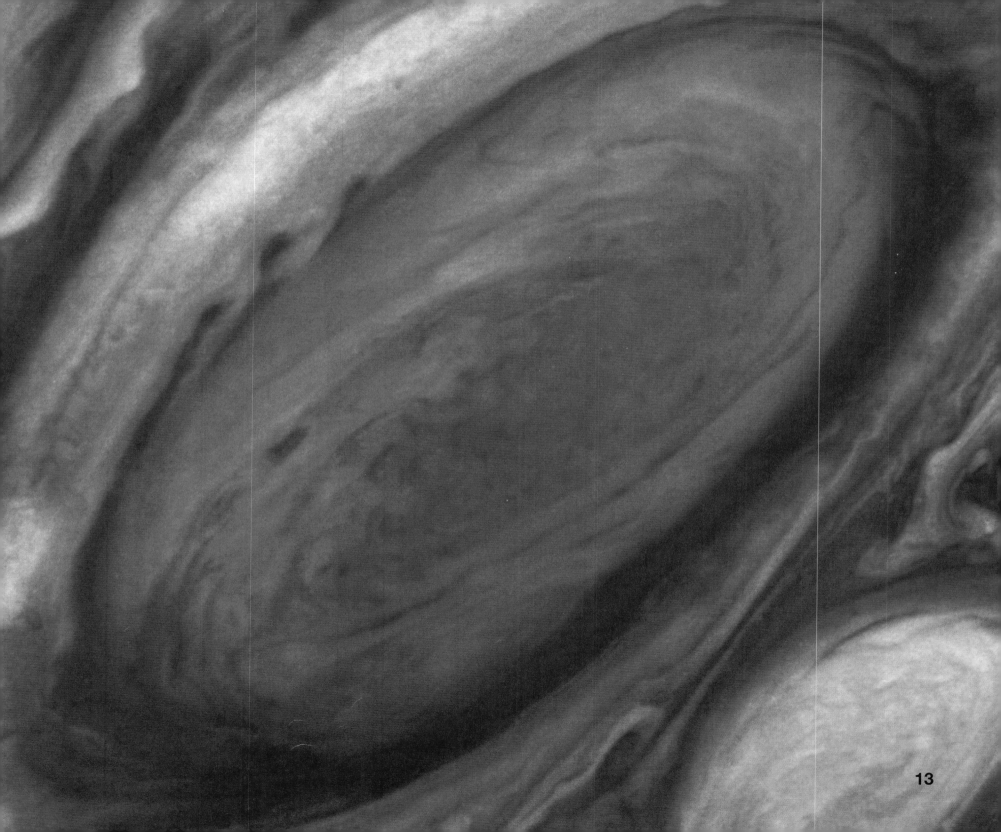

13

Jupiter's Size

Jupiter is much bigger
than Earth. Jupiter is
bigger than all of the
other planets put together.

El tamaño de Júpiter

Júpiter es mucho más grande
que la Tierra. Júpiter es
más grande que todos
los planetas juntos.

Earth/La Tierra

Jupiter's Moons

Jupiter has at least

47 moons. Earth has

only one moon.

Las lunas de Júpiter

Júpiter tiene por lo menos

47 lunas. La Tierra sólo tiene

una luna.

four of Jupiter's moons

cuatro de las lunas de Júpiter

People and Jupiter

People could not breathe

the air on Jupiter. Most

of the air is very thick.

La gente y Júpiter

En Júpiter la gente no podría

respirar el aire. La mayor

parte del aire es muy espeso.

People can see Jupiter
from Earth. Jupiter looks
like a bright star.

Desde la Tierra la gente
puede ver a Júpiter. Júpiter
parece una estrella brillante.

Jupiter/Júpiter

Glossary

breathe—to take air in and out of the lungs; people and animals must breathe to live.

gas—a substance, such as air, that spreads to fill any space that holds it; Jupiter is made mostly of gases.

moon—an object that moves around a planet; Io, Europa, Ganymede, and Callisto are Jupiter's largest moons.

planet—a large object that moves around the Sun; Jupiter is the fifth planet from the Sun.

solar system—the Sun and the objects that move around it; our solar system has nine planets and many moons, asteroids, and comets.

spacecraft—a vehicle that travels in space

star—a large ball of burning gases in space

Sun—the star that the planets move around; the Sun provides light and heat for the planets.

Glosario

estrella—una bola enorme de gases ardientes en el espacio

gas—una sustancia, como el aire, que se extiende hasta llenar el espacio que la contiene; en gran parte Júpiter está formado por gases.

luna—un objeto que se mueve alrededor de un planeta; Io, Europa, Ganímedes y Calisto son las lunas más grandes de Júpiter.

nave espacial—un vehículo que navega en el espacio

planeta—un objeto grande que se mueve alrededor del Sol; Júpiter es el quinto planeta a partir del Sol.

respirar—meter y sacar aire de los pulmones; la gente y los animales tienen que respirar para poder vivir.

sistema solar—el Sol y los objetos que se mueven a su alrededor; nuestro sistema solar tiene nueve planetas y muchas lunas, asteroides y cometas.

Sol—la estrella alrededor de la cual se mueven los planetas; el Sol proporciona luz y calor a los planetas.

Internet Sites

Do you want to find out more about Jupiter and the solar system? Let FactHound, our fact-finding hound dog, do the research for you.

Here's how:

1) Visit *www.facthound.com*

2) Type in the **Book ID** number: **0736821120**

3) Click on **FETCH IT.**

FactHound will fetch Internet sites picked by our editors just for you!

Sitios de Internet

¿Quieres saber más sobre Júpiter y el sistema solar? Deja que FactHound, nuestro perro sabueso, haga la investigación por ti.

Así:

1) Ve a *www.facthound.com*

2) Teclea el número ID del libro: **0736821120**

3) Clic en **FETCH IT.**

¡Facthound buscará en los sitios de Internet que han seleccionado nuestros editores sólo para ti!